Voyage

TOLU' A. AKINYEMI

First published in Great Britain as
a softback original in 2024

Copyright © Tolu' A. Akinyemi
The moral right of the author has been asserted.
All rights reserved.

No part of this publication may be reproduced, stored in a retrieval system, or transmitted, in any form or by any means, without the prior permission in writing of the author, nor be otherwise circulated in any form of binding or cover other than that in which it is published and without a similar condition including this condition being imposed on the subsequent purchaser.

Cover Design: Christopher Cook

Published by 'The Roaring Lion Newcastle'

ISBN: 978-1-913636-46-3
eISBN: 978-1-913636-47-0

Email:
author@tolutoludo.com
tolu@toluakinyemi.com

Website:
www.tolutoludo.com
www.toluakinyemi.com

ALSO, BY Tolu' A. Akinyemi from
The Roaring Lion Newcastle'

"Dead Lions Don't Roar" (A collection of Poetic
Wisdom for the Discerning, Series 1)
"Unravel your Hidden Gems" (A collection of
inspirational and motivational essays)
"Dead Dogs Don't Bark" (A collection
of Poetic Wisdom for the Discerning, Series 2)
"Dead Cats Don't Meow" (A collection
of Poetic Wisdom for the Discerning, Series 3)
"Never Play Games with the Devil" (A collection of poems)
"A Booktiful Love" (A collection of poems)
"Inferno of Silence" (A collection of short stories)
"Black ≠ Inferior" (A collection of poems)
"Never Marry A Writer" (A collection of poems)
"Everybody Don Kolomental" (A collection of poems)
"I Wear Self-Confidence Like a Second Skin" (Children's literature)
"I am Not a Troublemaker" (Children's literature)
"Born in Lockdown" (A collection of poems)
"A god in a Human Body" (A collection of poems)
"If You Have To Be Anything, Be Kind" (Children's literature)
"City of Lost Memories" (A collection of poems)
"Awaken Your Inner Lion" (A collection of essays)
"On The Train To Hell" (A collection of poems)
"You Need More Than Dreams" (A collection of poems)
"The morning Cloud is Empty" (A collection of poems)
"Architects of a Cleaner Financial System" (A collection of financial crime compliance poems)

PREFACE

The inspiration for this poetry chapbook came on a Sunday afternoon sometime in August 2023.

I was having a light-hearted conversation with a mentee of mine, who happens to be a poet, too. I was inspired by the funny context of our conversation that Sunday afternoon, and that sparked off the first poems in this chapbook.

This chapbook means a lot to me, as I was going through a dry writing spell at the time—not because of every writer's albatross (writer's block), but because I had a lot of other things going on in my literary life, like an upcoming tour and events on the horizon. Life itself is a "voyage," an expedition which has a beginning and an end. This chapbook of love poems explores the voyage of love in the context of true love, heartbreak, and many other facets of love.

Also, this is my first book that explores the theme of love as its sole purpose. I hope this book will find its lovers and readers who will treasure the gems inside its pages. Whether you're looking for love or have just survived a heartbreak, I hope you'll enjoy reading this chapbook, the latest addition to my glittering literary career.

Dedication

To everyone on the voyage of discovery for love, true love, that is calming like the sea.

Acknowledgements

Sincere appreciation to my darling wife Olabisi, for your support on my literary journey. Special thanks to my charmazing children Isaac and Abigail Akinyemi. Thanks for being my cheerleaders and supporting me wholeheartedly on this booktiful literary journey.

Heartfelt appreciation to my poetry editor, Jen Campbell – thank you for the duty of care while editing this poetry chapbook.

Thank you to Diane Donovan for a final proofread of this poetry chapbook.

To everyone who has supported me on my journey to literary acclaim – your support is greatly appreciated.

Contents

Let's Begin 1
Devouring 2
Burning 3
Sweet Words 4
Our Love 5
We Speak the Same Language 6
Spinster 7
A Write-Off 8
Manchester 9
Amber 10
Old Love 11
Faux Writer 12
Morpeth 13
This Is the Sign of Love.............................. 14
Play Right 15
Plot Twist 16
Memoriam 17
Caution 18
Breakfast 19
Two-Faced 20
Treacherous Love 21
Fictional 22
Onward 23
Light 24
Choices 25
Used 26
Mortality 27
Author's Note 29
Author's Bio 31
Dead Lions Don't Roar 35
Inferno of Silence 37

Let's Begin

This is a voyage of words.
        Little words,   *flowery words.*
Healing, soothing words knitting
broken hearts and art.

This is a sea of words.
        Floating,   *swimming*
through the foray of darkness.
Wrecking boats and dreams.

This is a river of words.
        Flooding,   *sweeping*
through my heart;
planting the idea of your love in me.

Devouring

I'm consuming your presence as a meal
before you become the wind.

I'm consuming your presence as a silent night
before the daybreak.

I'm consuming your presence as oxygen
before my lifeline vanishes into cloud.

Burning

I lay on my bed tonight,
engulfed by my own fantasies.

My heart is catching fire
with the remembrance of you.

I am on fire,
but your voice rides the calming waters

as the flames of love
envelope my soul.

Sweet Words

My girlfriend says my mouth is a sack of sugar
flavoured like the best sweeteners.

Who is a poet
without the mastery of language
tugging at the heart?

On and off:
           the page
           the stage
and everywhere in between.

Our Love

Our hearts were bound by chemistry;
biology's fatal attraction.

Our love was a work of fiction
kept afloat by imagined physics.

We Speak the Same Language

Speak the dialect of love.
Do not conform to the echoes
of mere mortals. This is our sacred ritual.

Speak the dialect of love
which ricochets beyond echo chambers
when words are buried in silent heaps.

Speak the dialect of love
when emotions become blurred
and the heart is filled with fragmented sounds.

Spinster

My girlfriend wants to marry a poet;
be swept off her feet by flowery words; whisked
away to Jupiter and Mars
before she is brought down to earth.

My girlfriend sashays to the words of a bard.
Who doesn't want to be nudged into paradise?

My girlfriend is still looking for a poet.
And a man.
And a poet.
And a man.
And a poet.
And any man
who will remove her from the rack of
spinsterhood.

A Write-Off

My first adventure on Bumble was a car crash.
The first swipe was a certified disaster.

I'm the parody of a neighbourhood poet.

There is no manual for flirting
or seeking new friendships
even for faithful partners
and lovers.

We are all seekers
of unfulfilled fantasies;
those sweet cravings
that might leave a bitter aftertaste.

Manchester

I remember that city,
and my woman friend
who told her boyfriend she was in love
with a married man.

He asked, 'Are you sure that he is married?'
'Yes,' she replied, sounding unbothered.
Who says married men can't plant
love splinters in the hearts of spinsters?

Amber

My therapist cannot keep a home.
Or a woman.

My counsellor is a ship
on cruise control.

My counsellor is an aeroplane.
on autopilot

rocked by self-inflicted turbulence;
about to crash into the pitch dark.

My therapist is a vulnerable boy—
one who needs therapy.

Old Love

I'm not a sugar daddy. I have no protruding
belly to show off my waning years.
My wealth is planted in uncashed assets
that would take an age to harvest.

I have neither gold nor fine ornaments—
just an overflowing river of words
to turn your heart
into a flowerbed.

Let me be your old love,
man of little money;
cache of words
manning your artillery till death do us part.

Faux Writer

She sent me a love poem
written by a ghostwriter.
Little wonder the words didn't move me.
I am unfazed by parodies;
by ghosts and their
pretences.

Morpeth

Hopeless romantic
sing like a canary.
I am laying eggs on this virgin island.

Weave words on this nested heart.
Let me be the picture-perfect
love of your fantasy.

Like Morpeth,
let me be the town of your dreams.

This Is the Sign of Love

The flawless innocence of your heart
washes every stretch of guilt.

This is the hallmark of love:
the immaculate freshness of your laughter,
semantics saturating like old wine.

This is the signpost of love:
the calming nature of your voice which
fills me with the strength of a battalion.

Play Right

Sometimes, I imagine I am greater than Shakespeare,
unearthing hidden diamonds
lying dormant in my underbelly.

Would you play right and be my Juliet? And I
will be the Romeo reincarnate.

They say it was written in the stars,
but who's the one that holds the pen?

Plot Twist

Her mood swings like Manchester's weather,
melancholic in nature:
a twisting tale.

How do we plot these characters
from Cinderella to an understudy?

The sequence of events is too bleak
to be waved off as a mere coincidence.

This plot is grim,
teetering on a bitter ending.

Memoriam

I sang a memorial hymn for our love—
a super love
that caught eyes
and ears;

one that filled the mouths of strangers
with lucid tales
and made others wish for our love;
this super love.

I wrote a dirge for our love,
our celestial love
constructed in the heavens.
This was a paradise — an unbelievable tale.

Caution

The sign reads:
tread with caution.
Don't date a poet
or a typewriter,
whether epistles or the brevity of language.
Poets spill things, and our little secrets
could be news screamers.
This affection is time-bound.
There is an accident lurking.
This love is on the knife-edge.
The road of love is slippery.
Would you open your eyes and read?

Breakfast

I was served a cold breakfast
from sour love's menu
at a high-end restaurant on Victoria Island.

I was served heartbreak,
cold as a dog's nose.

Two-Faced

My hands are snow white
like my heart.
The algorithm is stacked against me
like her words.
The conjectures are an illusion
like her thoughts.
I am spending my get-out-of-jail card
like an unseen ghost.
My hands are snow white
like my heart.

Treacherous Love

Your love language is hail
raining thunder
breaking things
colliding with beautiful memories.

This public display of affection
is a head-turner.
I'm masquerading pain.
Heavy, a burdensome load.
I have coated my face in hazardous paint
for this bal masque.

Fictional

Don't take my poems seriously
when the brain is working overtime,
stringing words together, ideating
in imagination squares.

Don't take my words seriously.
I'm a master wordsmith,
washing hearts in immaculate
prose and poetry.

Don't take me seriously.
I'm a work of fiction
which is out of character.

Onward

The voyage of life
and love is a drama-filled soap.
True love needs no embellishment.

The voyage of love
and life cannot be plagiarised
literally/literarily.

Like
> love languages
> unspeakable love,
> the comeuppance of treacherous love,

the voyage of life
is an ark of dreams
floating and fleeting.

I'm banking on the currency of my ancestors
for a long stretch
on this winding road.

But, oh! The ship has berthed on the dock,
and the clock
has come to a screeching halt.

Light

For Ilerioluwa Oladimeji Aloba (8 June 1996 – 12 September 2023), known professionally
as MohBad.

This is a heartbreak poem.
The eyes float in water.

This poem breaks hearts — like your passing
broke your artistry into a memorial song.

We have summoned the gods
                              for vengeance.
Our cries for justice have hit
a wall of deafening silence.

This city swallows its young;
oppresses them into cold silence.
This city swallows dreams;
suppresses them, stillborn.

Let there be light,
even in this dreaded night
as evil gusts swallow your burning lamp and
leave us with a fog as remembrance.

Choices

We are children of life's circumstances
afflicted by choices
good or bad.

I time-travelled onto the road not taken.
I'll treasure this;

this fragile love
far better than the dark alleys of my
imagination.

Used

I no longer fall for flattery
or flirtatious instincts.
I have fallen prey
to users
who end up losers.

Now I pray.

I have fallen
into the pit of unconditional love;
sacrificed that which was precious.

Now I trust my instincts
to weed out the shaft
springing on the window of my heart.

Mortality

I have fallen in love with my mortality;
accepted its terms and conditions
like those who came before those who came before.
One day, these booktiful chapters will be forever closed,
told as a folklore, and I will be buried
in Newcastle-Upon-Tyne,
the city of my shining star.
I'll lay like a log, clutching at my books
in solitude.
The atmosphere will be thick with roars;
intense like thunder and poetic renditions.
My tombstone will read:
The Lion of Newcastle - A Booktiful Author Story.
A statue will be erected in my honour in my hometown.
I have love for myself.
I have come to grips with my mortality
and I no longer fear death.

Voyage

Author's Note

Thank you for the time you have taken to read this book. I hope you enjoyed the poems in it.

If you loved the book and have a minute to spare, I would appreciate a short review on the page or site where you bought it. I greatly appreciate your help in promoting my work. Reviews from readers like you make a huge difference in helping new readers choose a book.

Thank you!
Tolu' A. Akinyemi

Voyage

Author's Bio

Tolu' A. Akinyemi (also known as Tolutoludo & the Lion of Newcastle) is a multiple award-winning author in the genres of poetry, short stories, children's literature, and essays.

His works include: Dead Lions Don't Roar (poetry, 2017); Unravel Your Hidden Gems (essays, 2018); Dead Dogs Don't Bark (poetry, 2018); Dead Cats Don't Meow (poetry, 2019); Never Play Games With the Devil (poetry, 2019); Inferno of Silence (short stories, 2020); A Booktiful Love (poetry, 2020); Black ≠ Inferior (poetry, 2021); Never Marry a Writer (poetry, 2021); Everybody Don Kolomental (poetry, 2021); I Wear Self-Confidence Like a Second Skin (children's literature, 2021); I Am Not a Troublemaker (children's literature, 2021); Born in Lockdown (poetry, 2021); A god in a Human Body (poetry, 2022); If You Have To Be Anything, Be Kind (children's literature, 2022); City of Lost Memories, (poetry, 2022); Awaken Your Inner Lion, (essays, 2022); On The Train To Hell, (poetry, 2022); You Need More Than Dreams (poetry, 2023); The Morning Cloud is Empty (poetry, 2023); and Architects of a Cleaner Financial System (poetry, 2023).

A former headline act at Great Northern Slam, Havering Literary Festival, Crossing The Tyne Festival, Feltonbury Arts and Music Festival, The Stanza, and The Cooking Pot, he also inspires large audiences through spoken word performances and has appeared as a keynote speaker in major forums and events. He facilitates creative writing master classes for many audiences.

His poems have appeared (or are forthcoming) in the 57th issue (Volume 15, No. 1) of the Wilderness House Literary Review; The Writers Cafe Magazine Issue 18; GN Books; Lion and Lilac; Agape Review; Continue the Voice; My Woven Poetry; Black Moon Magazine; Calla Press; African Writer Magazine; Football in Poetry 2 Anthology; and elsewhere.

His poems have been translated into Greek.

Tolu's poetry collection 'Everybody Don Kolomental' has been used as a teaching resource to engage with medical students in discussions about mental health and well-being at the University of Benin/Teaching Hospital, Edo-State, Nigeria. Also, his poem "Everybody don Kolomental," was read and analysed as a case study by Professor Kingsley Oalei Akhigbe, Professor of Psychiatry, in the 293rd Inaugural Lecture Series at the University of Benin, on the topic 'Kolomental and the Elephant in the Room - Our Mental Health.'

His books are based on a deep reality and often reflect relationships and life, featuring people he has met in his journey as a writer. His books have inspired many people to improve their performances and/or their circumstances. Tolu' has taken his poetry to the stage, performing his written word at many events. Through his writing and these performances, he supports business leaders, other aspiring authors, and people of all ages who are interested in reading and writing. Sales of the books have allowed Tolu' donate to charity, allowing him to make a difference where he feels it's important and showing that he lives by the words he puts to page.

He is a co-founder of Lion and Lilac, a UK-based arts organisation, and sits on the board of many organisations.

Tolu' is a financial crime compliance consultant as well as a Certified Anti-Money Laundering Specialist (CAMS) with extensive experience working with leading investment banks and consultancy firms.

He is a trained economist from Ekiti State University, formerly known as University of Ado-Ekiti (UNAD).

He sat for his master's degree in Accounting and Financial Management at the University of Hertfordshire, Hatfield, United Kingdom.

Tolu' was a student ambassador at the University of Hertfordshire, Hatfield, representing the university in major forums and engaging with young people during various assignments.

Tolu' Akinyemi was born in Ado-Ekiti, Nigeria and lives in the United Kingdom. Tolu' is an ardent supporter of Chelsea Football Club in London.

You can connect with Tolu' on his various social media accounts:

Instagram: @tolutoludo
Facebook: facebook.com/toluaakinyemi
Twitter: @ToluAkinyemi @tolutoludo

Dead Lions Don't Roar

In a society where moral rectitude is increasingly becoming abeyant, Akinyemi's bounden duty is to reawaken it with verse. He, thus, functions as a philosopher-poet, a kind of factotum inculcating wisdom in different facets of life. 'Dead Lions Don't Roar' leads us into the universe of an exact mind rousing the lethargic from indolence or prevarication, bearing in mind that the greatest achievers are those who take the bull by the horn. Taking a step can just be the open sesame to reach the stars. Enough of jeremiad! - **The Sun**

Dead Lions Don't Roar, a collection of poetic wisdom for the discerning, makes an interesting read. A paperback, the poems are concise, easy to digest, travel friendly and express deep feelings and noble thoughts in beautiful and simple language. **-The Nation**

Akinyemi's verses are concise, straight-edged and explanatory, reminiscent of the kind of poetry often churned out by Mamman J. Vatsa, the late soldier and poet. **–yNaija**

Dead Lion's Don't Roar is a collection of inspiring and motivating modern-day verses. Addressing many issues close to home and also many taboo subjects, the poetry is reflective of today's struggles and lights the way to a positive future. The uplifting book will appeal to all age groups and anyone going through change, building or enjoying a career, and facing day to day struggles. Many of the short verses will resonate with readers, leaving a sense of peace and wellbeing.

Inferno of Silence

Inferno of Silence is a wide-ranging collection that tackles different themes of love, life, interpersonal relationships, and social and political challenges. It's a hard-hitting, revealing collection that keeps readers engaged and thinking with each short exploration of characters who confront their prejudices, realities, and the winds of change in their lives.

Readers of literary explorations that include African cultural influence and modern-day dilemmas will find this collection engrossing. - **D. Donovan, Senior Reviewer, Midwest Book Review**

Poignant and honest...
Akinyemi's first collection of short stories dazzles with elegant prose, genuine emotions, and Nigerian cultural lore as it plumbs both the socio-cultural issues and the depths of love, loss, grief, and personal trauma. Lovers of literary fiction will be rewarded. - **The Prairies Book Review**

The first collection of short stories by this multitalented author entwines everyday events that are articulated in excellent storytelling.

The title story "Inferno of Silence" portrays men's societal challenges and the unspoken truths and burdens that men bear, while "Black lives Matter" shows the firsthand trauma of a man facing racism as a footballer plying his trade in Europe.

Stories range from "Return Journey" where we encounter a techpreneur/ Poet/Serial Womanizer confronting consequences of his past actions, to "Blinded by Silence," where a couple united by love must face a political upheaval changing their fortune.

These are completed with stories of relationships: "Trouble in Umudike" – about family wealth and marriage; "Everybody Don Kolomental" where the main character deals with mental health issues; and "In the Trap of Seers" when one's life is on auto-reverse with the death of her confidante, her mother, as she takes us through her ordeal and journey to redemption. This is a broad and very inclusive collection.

Voyage

Voyage

www.ingramcontent.com/pod-product-compliance
Lightning Source LLC
Chambersburg PA
CBHW030134100526
44591CB00009B/657